YOUR KNOWLEDGE H

- We will publish your bachelor's and master's thesis, essays and papers

- Your own eBook and book - sold worldwide in all relevant shops

- Earn money with each sale

Upload your text at www.GRIN.com and publish for free

Nicole Schindler, Julia Oesterreich

The new women movement of the 1890s in England

GRIN Verlag

Bibliografische Information der Deutschen Nationalbibliothek:

Die Deutsche Bibliothek verzeichnet diese Publikation in der Deutschen National-
bibliografie; detaillierte bibliografische Daten sind im Internet über http://dnb.d-
nb.de/ abrufbar.

Imprint:

Copyright © 2005 GRIN Verlag GmbH
Druck und Bindung: Books on Demand GmbH, Norderstedt Germany
ISBN: 978-3-638-84351-5

This book at GRIN:

http://www.grin.com/en/e-book/47197/the-new-women-movement-of-the-1890s-
in-england

GRIN - Your knowledge has value

Der GRIN Verlag publiziert seit 1998 wissenschaftliche Arbeiten von Studenten, Hochschullehrern und anderen Akademikern als eBook und gedrucktes Buch. Die Verlagswebsite www.grin.com ist die ideale Plattform zur Veröffentlichung von Hausarbeiten, Abschlussarbeiten, wissenschaftlichen Aufsätzen, Dissertationen und Fachbüchern.

Visit us on the internet:

http://www.grin.com/

http://www.facebook.com/grincom

http://www.twitter.com/grin_com

Content Overview

1. The New Woman - An Introduction

2. The New Woman's Name and Means
2.1 The New Woman's Image

3. New Education

4. The New Woman Literature

5. Challenges of and to Fashion

6. The New Woman's Take on the 'Woman Question'

7. The New Woman and Sexuality
7.1 Lesbianism

8. Conclusion

The Eighteen-Nineties: New Women

1. The New Woman – An Introduction

This paper will look at the New Woman movement of the 1890s in England. The Fin de Siècle was full of new ideas and challenges. Exciting social and technical developments and inventions took place. Women had challenged their subordinate social and political positions and condemned prevailing sexual double standard throughout the course of the 19th century. Feminists and advocates for the 'Woman Cause' urged for women's rights to employment and full citizenship. In the last ten years of the century, though, the fight for liberation and achievement went a step further. Personal decisions, like dress, habit, choice of partner, or occupation were now becoming increasingly political. The women who fought on the frontlines, and were therefore the movement's most visible agents, were referred to as New Women. The struggle was not only carried out on an individual level. In the 1850s, women had begun to organise in groups in order to question and defy their subordinate position in society. They were starting to agitate and speak out on all kinds of fields in culture and politics. Feminists were able to profit from the 1890's accelerated speed of cultural developments; hitherto unthinkable things were being talked about in the press, in women's clubs, in non-fictional and fictional books, even in fashion magazines. We will explore a variety of these new social and literary forms the New Woman movement in England adopted at the end of the 19th century.

Furthermore we will discuss the different contemporary debates on femininity. A special focus will be on the views on sexuality, the concept of marriage, and lesbianism at the time. Gender dynamics as well as social norms, laws, and professional options for women dramatically changed during the last ten years of the century. New theories on Darwin's ideas, exploration into the field of psychology, as well as pure pragmatics all shaped the discourse.

The New Women were by no means a homogenous group. We will highlight some of the members' various political ideas on education, marriage laws and social morality, and discuss their cultural achievements.

One of the main questions in this paper will be: Did the new woman movement really bring about a new type of woman? Did the new women movement make any real changes? If so, what were the limits?

2. The New Woman's Name and Means

It was Ouida (pen name of the English novelist Maria Louise Ramé), storywriter and novelist, who took the now famous phrase 'the new woman' from British author and activist Sarah Grand's essay ' The New Aspect of the Woman Question'. With this term she wanted to give those power-seeking females of her times, who were prepared to overturn conventions and accepted notions of femininity, a name. These women showed their 'emancipation' in every day life through practices like, for example, smoking, riding bicycles, using bold language or taking the omnibus or train unescorted. They sometimes belonged to all-female clubs like "Mrs. Massingberd's Pioneer Club" or societies where like-minded individuals met and interchanged ideas. New Women wanted their own careers, desired sexual liberation from male suppression, and proper laws against marital violence.

The New Woman movement was a social and literary phenomenon and is generally considered the predecessor of the suffrage movement.[1] Due to this movement, the latter half of the 19th century saw passionate discussions and agitation on matters such as marriage and divorce laws, women's property and custody rights, educational and employment opportunities for women as well as a lively debates on female suffrage.

When looking at these discussions one needs to differentiate between two generations of New Women, the first around the 1880s and 1890s and the second around the 1920s and the 1930s. In our paper we will concentrate on the first generation.

At a first glance middle-class New Women agitated primarily for changes in etiquette. They wanted an end to chaperones, long hair, and long skirts. At a second look they, more importantly, also fought for graver matters such as extended professional opportunities, a chance to safe independent travel and living, and the right to choose one's partner(s). They fought for these changes in the popular press; often in the same magazines that at other times portrayed New Women as "unsexed, terrifying, violent Amazon(s) ready to overturn the world"[2]. In the field of fiction writing the engaged women could express challenging ideas more freely. Non-fictional writing also helped to voice matters not dared to be mentioned publicly before. The suffragette movement depended in particular on such publications.

Women also gained access to printing houses. Feminist newspapers of the 1890s such as "Shaft" and "The Woman's Signal" persistently gave voice to the New Woman's concerns when such voices were heard only sporadically in more mainstream journals. Some critics

---

[1]see: http://www.historylearningsite.co.uk/suffragettes.htm
[2] Richardson, Angelique (ed.). *The New Woman in Fiction and in Fact*: Fin-de-Siècle Feminisms, S. 39

claim that literature and fiction had never before contributed so much to the feminist movement as it did at the fin de siècle. To a certain extent the history of the New Woman is only available textually, since the "New Woman" was largely a discursive phenomenon. By naming themselves, New Women opened up their discursive space in the public. This space was quickly filled by feminist textual productions of feminist activists, female social reformers, female popular novelists, female suffragette play writers, and woman poets who valued self-fulfillment and believed in legal and sexual equality. New Women themselves did not always define their goals clearly, their fiction, for example, reveals complexities and contradictions which withstand reductive readings.

2.1 The New Woman's Image

The first descriptions of the New Women emerged in the press in the early 1890s. The satirical magazine "Punch", for example, presented an image of a woman with the "typical" features of a spinster wearing glasses, trousers and a short haircut, which was seemingly envious of lovely fashionable ladies, and labelled it "The New Woman". This image of the New Woman, a newly perceived form of femininity, developed further during the next years. The symbolism was clear to readers of the time. When pictures showed a woman with a latchkey, this then stood for the challenging independence these New Women claimed for themselves, because it enabled them to come and go from their apartment (or the apartment of their husbands) as they pleased. On other pictures we see a "New Woman" smoking a cigarette, which at that time was an exclusively male habit. All in all, these pictures ascribed "more opinions, positions, and beliefs [to the women of the feminist movement] than any real woman could have absorbed in a lifetime.[3]" "Punch" exemplified this notion probably best through its 1894 portray of the 'Donna Quixote'[4] – a seemingly powerful and independent woman with latchkey and cigarette with glasses who reads and sits in a kind of throne. In the background the observer can see - amongst others – the reproduction of a female soldier with a male head lying at her feet, the inscription reads 'tyrant man'. Books by Mona Caird, a feminist journalist of the time, by the then scandalous Norwegian playwright Henrik Ibsen, and Russian writer Leo Tolstoy complete the "Punch" caricature. The placing of allegedly subversive books in that picture is telling. Many conservatives considered higher education

---

[3] Richardson, Angelique (ed.). *The New Woman in Fiction and in Fact*: Fin-de-Siècle Feminisms, S.50
[4] see: "Donna Quixote" in "Punch", 28 April 1894 zit. in *A New Woman Reader*, S. 228

not only unnecessary but also even dangerous for women. Also the notion that these new ideas come from outside of England is equally interesting. We will go into further detail on the subject of literacy and literature in the following paragraphs.

All of these particularities did mark the New Woman as independent and thereby also possibly threatening to the established societal rules or at least suspicious with respect to her intents. Therefore, what writers and readers at the fin de siècle thought the New Woman was, the way in which she was constructed by and was a product of discourse, is just as 'real' and historically significant as the factual lives of New Women.

New Women were sometimes called "wild women" by the media. In articles it was insinuated that they opposed marriage and sought personal independence and political rights through power over men. In many portrays, this new type of woman was pictured as morally decadent, mannish, asexual but also sexually lecherous. Magazines like "Punch", some ladies' magazines or even the literary journal "The Yellow Book", the major platform for aestheticist artists, blamed new practices in the education of women for the evolvement of these New Women and their supposed 'masculinisation' through it.

Even though these pictures were often caricatures and highly exaggerated, they did partly reflect reality. Many of the New Women around the 1890s were young, single middle class women who eschewed the fripperies of fashion in favor of more masculine dress.[5] They often were educated to a standard unknown to previous generations of women. They engaged in occupations, past-times, and habits of behavior that were hitherto only thought suitable for male citizens.

---

[5] see: http://www.tudorlinks.com/treasury/articles/view1890.html

3. New Education

The foundation of new educational opportunities for women was one of the major areas of the new feminist activity. By the 1890s universal elementary schooling had been in existence, legally at least, for two full decades and many new and academically competent private schools for girls had been founded. Established women's colleges were awarding degrees to women and some female scholars could train at women's medical colleges in London and Edinburgh, which had been established by the pioneer women doctors of the previous years. New Women saw education as the key to a broad range of other freedoms. This attitude was also reflected in their habit of reading 'advanced' books usually read only by men and in their stance towards work. The New Woman sought to be financially independent of husband or father through earning her own living in one of the career opportunities opening up to women at the time, like journalism or teaching. "Between 1851 and 1901 the total number of women in the workforce increased from 2.832.000 to 4.751.000."[6], this number includes all the women who were answering industrialisation's demand for cheap manual labour, paid work for women with a higher education was still sparse.

4. The New Woman Literature

Literary scholars established two epochs of New Woman writers, which can be aligned with the women's rights movements of that time. The decade around 1890 is called the first epoch, it saw many new female writers emerge (like George Egerton); others were already moderately established but produced their most interesting works in that period. Sarah Grand and Olive Schreiner can be counted into that last group. The second wave started in the late 1920s, when authors such as Virginia Woolf, Djuna Barnes, or Radclyffe Hall came onto the scene. With the beginning of the Second World War, the voices of female as well as male writers grew weaker. This is one of the reasons the end of that second epoch is set at around 1940.

Male writers also represented the New Woman in fiction. In the last decade of the century novelists began representing the "new woman" as a character type. The most famous example is Sue Bridehead in Thomas Hardy's *Jude the Obscure* (1896). Another example is George Gissing's *The Odd Women* (1893), or women without husbands. Gissing's novel traces the fortunes of five "odd women," who make their own living. One of them, Mary Barfoot, uses

---

[6] Richardson, Angelique (ed.). *The New Woman in Fiction and in Fact*: Fin-de-Siècle Feminisms, S.5

her modest inheritance to train women for work in offices and persuade them of the importance of a women's revolution. Grant Allen's *The Woman Who Did* (1895) also takes up the theme of an independent, young, middle-class woman. Her suicide in reaction to her only child's shame about the mother's unmarried state leaves the reader with an ambiguous ending. Many critics of the time put this handling of the heroine's fate into the reactionary corner. Suicide or death is a recurring theme in New Woman novels. The insecurities coming with an independent life were treated as either surmountable or too frustrating to even start on liberation. The text's context and the author's intents give a clue to its possible reading.

New Women novels are not only important for the history of women's literature; they also reflect quite strikingly what was on women's minds at the fin de siècle. In their novels the authors urgently express late-Victorian women's increasing frustration with the constraints of the private sphere, additionally they also attempt to imagine new forms of living for women, which are not primarily defined by marriage. The hallmark of New Women fiction is an overtly political agenda: a focus on an independent woman seeking a career outside marriage. Many female authors of the time often argue strenuously for the values of social activism, literary or artistic ambition, and female friendship. New Women novels usually wanted women to be empowered with knowledge, most importantly about the female self, sex, and sexually transmitted diseases. Many writers believed that in order to attain this, writing novels might not be enough, that rather a reinvention of marriage was necessary. Although , the distinction between the real and the fictional world was never omitted, the boundaries and obstacles that were evident in the women's realities were sometimes transgressed in the novels' fictions. Although New Woman writers usually sent their heroine off to battle for survival in an urban space and many characters do daring things and manage to hold their own in the face of male adversity, they often end with the character's failure to accomplish her goal of reinventing society and finding her own rightful and satisfying place in it. The authors themselves on the other hand, often did manage to make a living by pursuing an artistic (or other) career, and individually came to terms with their own environment.

One of the new themes, the New Woman writers introduced were marital breakdown and remarriage. In 1881, French author Emile Zola complained that legalized divorce would be the ruin of literature because it would make marital misery solvable and thus rob the novelist of his [sic!] subject matter[7]. The New Woman novelists proved him wrong.

New Women novels are also important for another reason: they constitute an important set of proto-modernist innovations. New Women novelists used proto-modernist techniques: their

---

[7] Richardson, Angelique (ed.). *The New Woman in Fiction and in Fact*: Fin-de-Siècle Feminisms, p.61

writing were messier, more journalistic, more experimental, more multi-voiced, more diffuse, and more open-ended than most Victorian realism. The second epoch saw many of these techniques again taken up by writers such as Virginia Woolf. In Victorian fiction realism was the dominant mode of writing, yet New Women novelists often eschewed realism in favor of hallucinatory dream sequences or lyrical interludes or fragmentary glimpses of alternate modes (as incorporated by Sarah Grand, Olive Schreiner, George Egerton). They often shifted among different characters' points of view and wrote in the mode of personal confession and direct pleas, not omniscient narration. Mona Caird, among others, sometimes refused closure, leaving the characters suspended in their current lives. George Egerton saw her short stories as representing a symptomatic moment in an ongoing life. The New Women writers borrowed techniques from journalism: instead of trying to write dense, symbolic, allusive, timeless fiction, they prized urgency, transparency, and contemporaneity (Dixon, Caird, Iota). In their own lifetimes their innovations were often read as failures to emulate proper literature, but today, a century later, we can see them as important experimentalists.

George Egerton almost single-handedly introduced the short story into the British canon. It is no surprise that the short story triumphed at a time when sexual and social roles were in unprecedented confusion, because it was easier to raise new subjects in a new form. Eventually, the short story became the dominant literary form in Britain and in the United States at the close of the 19th century. Whatever their precise social and political agenda, women needed a new fiction if they were to break free from social, as well as literary, tradition, so women writers on both sides of the Atlantic were daringly experimenting with short stories, breaking out of tired literary codes, outgrowing happily-ever-after romances and questioning existing relationship patterns and sexualities.

Critics despised what they saw as the sloppy writing and undeserved sales of most New Women novelists, but a few received more respect from the literary establishment of the 1890s. Perhaps the most critically acclaimed of the New Woman novels was Olive Schreiner's *Story of an African Farm* (1883). Schreiner used innovative non-realist techniques to depict the tortured life of the independent woman Lyndall. The novel is scored with myth, fantasy, and dreams, and, like Sarah Grand's *The Heavenly Twins (1893)*, it includes a scene of cross-dressing, which undermines gender roles. Schreiner, a South African herself, used Africa not as an exotic backdrop but as a well-realized place, incorporating details of geography, customs, and language that carried their own fascinating verisimilitude for British readers. Although she published *Story of an African Farm* under a male pseudonym (Ralph Iron), the novel is now considered as one of the first pieces of feminist writing. George Egerton was also critically acclaimed for her two books of short stories, *Keynotes* and *Discords*. (1893, 1894). Both are innovative reinventions of the short story form, impressionistic and non-linear, fragmented, with multiple points of view, often giving no closure and refusing to answer the questions they evoked for what the authors wanted was an inner (in the - possibly female – reader) and a public discussion of matters that shaped the lives of more than half of the population.

5. Challenges of and to fashion

In Victorian times dress for women was still too stiff and ornamental to allow free body movement. In the 1890s this slowly began to change, although huge sleeves and the amount of fabric used would confine the wearer to certain movements. The fullness of the dress was drawn to the back of the waist, which produced a slim and perpendicular silhouette. The skirt remained free of trimming and instead the bodice was emphasised. The sleeves were the most important feature of the dress. The dress code became, on the one hand, extremely feminine in style, yet the skirt and the shoes were potentially more practical. Cross-dressing became another topic of feminist fiction.

Society's perception of two opposite genders determined the moral judgement about male and female actions. Through its development into a more masculine direction, cross-dressing served to destabilize the Victorian body politics. Furthermore transvestism disrupted the binary opposites, which structured the sexual and social order into sex and gender, male and female, and straight and gay. "By demonstrating the essential performance of gender, it enabled feminists to challenge biological notions of sexual difference deployed to rationalize women's political disempowerment as the 'product of nature'."[8]

Cross-dressing raised debates on androgyny.[9] While the public reaction to male (especially Oscar Wilde) and female cross-dressing was the same, the motivation behind it could vary considerably, depending on the sex and the sexual orientation of the wearer. Ann Heilmann argues that "if cross-dressing encoded sexual liberation for gay men, it appealed to many women primarily for economic and health reasons, and was adopted by feminist writers for its social and political implications.[10]"

For women cross-dressing brought a relief from physical pain, which was inflicted by the Victorian feminine dress code. Corsets were a health hazard, which could deform the

---

[8] Heilmann, Ann. *New woman fiction*: women writing first-wave feminism, S. 118
[9] see: Heilmann, Ann. *New woman fiction*: women writing first-wave feminism
[10] Heilmann, Ann. *New woman fiction*: women writing first-wave feminism, S. 131

skeleton, impair the blood circulation, cause respiratory problems, and could lead to irreversible damage of lung and liver[11]. Male cross-dressers, on the other hand, emphasized the sensual pleasure they got from wearing female clothes. For them it meant to "capture the elusive nature of femininity".[12]

Male writers presented the female cross-dresser as a "castrated, sexless, and sad neuter"[13] and sexologists and psychiatrists defined cross-dressing "as a clinical symptom of homosexuality, with men suffering from 'effemination' and women from 'viraginity'"[14] With comments like these sexologists blurred the differences between anatomical sex, socially constructed gender and individual sexual orientation. They feminized gay men and attributed stereotypical masculine traits to lesbians.

6. The New Women's Take On the 'Woman Question'

In the late 19th century new data suggested that women significantly outnumbered men in Great Britain. This meant that a certain number of women would not be able to marry; they were called the 'superfluous women' by the press. The dominant discourse at the time was that these 'superfluous women' would pose a threat to the tradition of marriage and to the separate sphere ideology. There had always been women who had not been married because of various reasons but for the first time in British history this number would be significantly large. The establishment responded to this Woman Question, as the phenomenon was called in the press, with a calling for all 'superfluous women' to emigrate and become wives of British men in the colonies.[15] New Women on the other hand requested proper education and employment opportunities for women so that they would be able to provide for themselves financially.

At the same time, there was a tremendous debate over whether women's 'natural role' was simply to procreate, or whether women should have the same range of choices as men. Conservatives warned that women who denied themselves the experience of becoming a mother were 'unsexing' themselves. This denial would bring forth horrendous physical and psychological consequences for the woman who failed to fulfill her predetermined task. New Women on the other hand insisted that they were more than breeding animals and praised the value of work as a fulfilling goal in itself. Anyhow, one has to see that the New Women were

---

[11] Heilmann, Ann. *New woman fiction*: women writing first-wave feminism, S. 127
[12] Heilmann, Ann. *New woman fiction*: women writing first-wave feminism, S. 127
[13] Heilmann, Ann. *New woman fiction*: women writing first-wave feminism, S. 125
[14] Heilmann, Ann. *New woman fiction*: women writing first-wave feminism, S.128
[15] see: Ledger, Sally. *The New Woman: Fiction and Feminism at the Fin de Siècle*

not one conform group but many different kinds of women with different ideas, viewpoints, and attitudes. Sarah Grand and Mona Caird, to name two great public figures of the time, had a debate on motherhood. Sarah Grand advocated sexual purity and motherhood in her book "The Heavenly Twins" whereas Mona Caird attacked these themes in her book "Daughters of Danaus". In her writing, motherhood is explored as a central site of female oppression and it is a symbol of enforced marital sex. Yet, Caird did not want to be associated with feminist essentialists, she, on the other hand, linked her vision of a socially caring society not to women's reproductive capacity but to the nurturing ability of both sexes. Earlier Women writers had highlighted motherhood and its controversies in a male-centered society and had often ended their novels with the death of the mother. In comparison, in New Women fiction mothers lived to tell their story. Motherhood furthermore developed to an emblem of moral and spiritual superiority, validating the feminist call for women's political and social leadership because their biological capacity to give birth made them in their views the superior sex. New Women fought against the subordination of women through motherhood in a late-Victorian patriarchal society in which motherhood was employed as a form of social control by linking reproduction to marriage and the duty of female self-sacrifice. The heroines of New Women fiction, and New Women themselves, responded to these pressures in different ways. Some married and had children and then started to rebel against their husbands, parents, and the society. Others rebelled by rejecting motherhood altogether or developed alternative models of mothering[16] like public childcare or living and sharing responsibilities in communes. Therefore the theme of motherhood can be interpreted as the means of a developing female body autonomy and self-consciousness. Male-controlled and socially imposed motherhood on the other hand was condemned in literature and everyday life since it created female subjection and alienation.

Anti-feminists feared that female emancipation would lead women to reject to give birth to children and become mothers. Therefore they demanded that women should not be formally educated but trained for 'femininity', which would evolve into a longing for the experience of motherhood. Male anti-feminist writers glorified motherhood in their fiction with the result that in many works fatherhood was radically decentred.[17]

Feminist writers often made failure of marriage and its sexual exploitation, violence, and transference of diseases like syphilis a theme of their writing. They suggested that the existing legislation did not go far enough and that it was an essential right of women to own and protect their own body. New Women demanded a social and marital restructuring that would

---

[16] see: Heilmann, Ann. *New woman fiction*: women writing first-wave feminism
[17] see: Heilmann, Ann. *New woman fiction*: women writing first-wave feminism

allow for an education in sexual matters of women before marriage and a change of the patriarchal concept of the 'beautiful innocence' of women[18]. This concept contained the fear that "impressionable feminine minds might be twisted beyond recall if they were told too much about male sexuality."[19] Feminists blamed the moral and legal double standard that regulated marriage and, for example, prostitution, for encouraging men's sexual exploitation of women. Middle-class women were defined "as the upholders of morality whose parameters they were denied a voice in shaping"[20] and many working-class women were cast as prostitutes and disciplined for corrupting and infecting men[21]. By keeping middle-class girls and women ignorant of vital sexual information concerning marriage and the fact that many men did have previous sexual experience, society in a way encouraged men's sexual exploits of women.

The sex education debate enabled feminist writers to deal with topics like rape in marriage in their fiction and furthermore to demand the women's right to own their bodies within marriage. In many of the feminist novels of the fin de siècle, New Women insisted that women who found themselves in a situation of legal prostitution created by their violent husbands or by suppressing social laws should leave the marriage. They plead for equal partnership in earning, decision-making, and domestic affairs.[22] In many novels, marriage or even a mere period of engagement results in women's mental and physical breakdown or leads to insanity or death of the woman. A recovery seems possibly only if women leave their husbands and live separately ('women-alone ending') or in co-habitation with women (marriage resistance as the cornerstone of female solidarity).[23]

Out of this developed the 'free love' theme in literature in which female characters break free from patriarchal control and both partners have autonomy and independence. Free love was defined "as the monogamous union of two individuals free from intrusive regulations by church and state.[24]" This could only be realized if both partners were financially independent. 'Free love' as a theme is complemented in New Woman fiction by the theme of female sexual transgression within marriage. Some novels envisioned experimental or utopian solutions like marriage in which partners live in separate flats or are prepared to accommodate other sexual partners, which challenged the late-Victorian ideas of female sexuality and conceptualized a

---

[18] Heilmann, Ann. *New woman fiction*: women writing first-wave feminism, S. 79
[19] Heilmann, Ann. *New woman fiction*: women writing first-wave feminism, S. 79
[20] Heilmann, Ann. *New woman fiction*: women writing first-wave feminism, S. 80
[21] see: Heilmann, Ann. *New woman fiction*: women writing first-wave feminism
[22] see: Ledger, Sally. *The New Woman: Fiction and Feminism at the Fin de Siècle*
[23] see: Heilmann, Ann. *New woman fiction*: women writing first-wave feminism
[24] Richardson, Angelique (ed.). *The New Woman in Fiction and in Fact*: Fin-de-Siècle Feminisms, S. 232

new kind of sexual relationship outside conventional marriage.[25] New Women who spoke out for free love, female sexual autonomy, and the realization of personal desires often argued that this individual development was only possible outside of marriage.

7. The New Woman and Sexuality

Feminists' struggle for women's rights went a step further with debates on gender and sexuality. New Women argued that gender was a social, not a biological, concept and tried to show that the sexes were essentially alike through, for example, cross-dressing. They suggested that women could become men if they wanted to and stated that the traditional notions of femininity were enforced by patriarchal ideas of medicine, family, and marriage. It was therefore costume, not body, which inscribed gender and assigned social power. These traditional concepts kept women subordinate to men and reduced them in a way to reproductive machines because the structures themselves regulated motherhood, created dependence, self-sacrifice, and domesticity for women. The dominant medico-scientific discourse for example focused on reproductive issues concerning women and critically emphasized the New Woman's supposed refusal of maternity, thereby leaving other, more important, themes like sexually transmitted diseases out of the discussion.

New Women found two ways to deal with the objectification of the female body. Women writers took the collective dissatisfaction with feminine role expectations up, turned the bodies of their heroines into a device of feminist resistance, and claimed body autonomy for themselves and their co-combatants.[26] The cross-dressing plot served to destabilize the categories of sexuality and gender. Additionally, New Women started to change the female dress code, which was one of the primary signifiers of femininity at the time and automatically inscribed biological differences between women and men.

Social purists, who emphasized the dangers rather than the pleasure of sex, claimed that civic responsibility and chastity for both sexes needed to be practiced in the interest of a healthy nation. The theme of sexuality was not talked about openly but transferred to other levels of conversation, be it national procreational statistics or the question of soldiers' state of health. The discourse was concentrated on men; female sexuality was perceived and taught to be virtually non-existent. Although there were women who were – in spite of the public discourse - conscious about their sexuality, the expression of it was highly suspicious and even dangerous. Whether women practiced a way of free love or preached sexual resistance,

---

[25] see: Heilmann, Ann. *New woman fiction*: women writing first-wave feminism
[26] see: Ledger, Sally. *The New Woman: Fiction and Feminism at the Fin de Siècle*

they were subjected to severe reprisal, and occasionally even to radical surgery[27]. The feminist call for male virtue and female celibacy must be seen in the context of institutionalized sexual violence against women. Women who (even in the privacy of their homes) displayed too much sexual pleasure were often reported to and treated by medical doctors. To counteract female resistance, or sexual practices that allegedly threatened masculinity, some physicians advised clitoridectomy. This brutal medical treatment was supposed to regulate women who had independent sexual urges (and confessed to have relieved this via masturbation) or who expressed their distaste for marital intercourse[28]. Clitoridectomy was deployed to suppress any form of female desire that was not directed towards men or reproduction and was practiced to discipline the unruly female body. In novels of the fin de siècle clitoridectomy was not mentioned because it was perceived as too unmentionable to be explored openly[29], but even though not written about directly, New Women fiction linked other forms of male violence with sexual violence against women (for example medical violence against animals). In second-wave feminist literature clitoridectomy is explicitly approached.

Against the background of female genital mutilation, it may not surprise that many women rejected sexual intercourse with men at the end of the 19th century. The exploitation and violation of many women lead to an atmosphere of aggression against men as the originators and perpetrators of this harsh medical treatment and to a fear of men. In literature some female writers showed new options like leaving the abusive husband and with him the threat of medical treatment for a life by oneself. Once this freedom was gained, other options for a fulfilled sexuality seemed possible. One of these was to enter an intimate relationship with another woman.

7.1 Lesbianism

Heterosexuality was held to be both normal and natural throughout the 19th century, but one can say that in the last two decades an increase in visible homosexuality could be witnessed. This development concerned mainly men and was found especially, but not exclusively, in the intelligentsia. Male homosexual activity was not illegal until 1885. That year sexual intercourse between two men in private became a criminal offence, which led for example to the imprisonment of Oscar Wilde in 1896. Female sexuality was supposed to be included in

---

[27] see: Ledger, Sally. *The New Woman: Fiction and Feminism at the Fin de Siècle*
[28] see: Ledger, Sally. *The New Woman: Fiction and Feminism at the Fin de Siècle*
[29] see: Heilmann, Ann. *New woman fiction*: women writing first-wave feminism,

the act of 1885 as well, but Queen Victoria declared it impossible for two women to be sexually active together, and it was omitted. This underlines the common ignorance about female sexuality. In the 1870s women's sexual activities could neither be criminalized nor called pathological, since they existed neither in law nor in medical textbooks.

Lesbianism was already being written about in fiction, but since these novels all came from France it were perceived as a typically French vice.[30] A first approach at talking about female homosexuality was undertaken when some British New Women wrote about heterosexuality as a collapsing phenomenon. Sexuality on the whole was a very difficult topic at the fin de siècle and heterosexuality was seen, because of its increasing association with rape and diseases, as intrinsically connected with germs and violence. The women writers portrayed sisterly intimacy, sisterhood, and female connectedness as more important and affectionate than sexual passion. A great number of stories by New Women featured same-sex relationships between women. What is striking though is that it is in novels by male writers of the time that New Women characters are called pathologically 'lesbian'. Women writers of feminist New Woman fiction preferred the term 'romantic friendship' for the female relationships in their fiction. This 'female relationship' model can already be found in sentimental literature of the 18th century, which had 'desexualized' the expression of physical affection in woman-to-woman friendships. The female principle of sisterhood was frequently comprised by the class divide between New Women and their protégées and thus social hierarchies in women's literature of the time remain largely unchallenged. Friendships developed only between New Women characters themselves who often came from the same middle- to upper class background.[31] Nonetheless these female friendships and the political sisterhood portrayed represented an important counter-plot to the conventional 'marriage-ending'.

Until the 1890s same-sex love between women had been regarded as a harmless and even healthy preparation for heterosexual love and marriage.[32] By general understanding, sexual intercourse for procreative purposes was the only kind of sexual activity imaginable for the 19th century woman and there were no existing concepts of sexual relationship between women. Middle-class 19th century women were believed to be asexual, consenting to heterosexual acts only to please their husbands and to have children. "This made it possible for women to form passionate and physically close friendships, sometimes to enter same-sex

[30] see: Ledger, Sally. *The New Woman: Fiction and Feminism at the Fin de Siècle*
[31] see: Heilmann, Ann. *New woman fiction*: women writing first-wave feminism
[32] see: Ledger, Sally. *The New Woman: Fiction and Feminism at the Fin de Siècle*

'marriage', which today would be regarded as lesbian."[33] There was a broadening awareness of lesbian love relationships amongst intellectuals from the 1880s on because there were some prominent female relationships. The question is if these supposed 'couples' were self-assertive lesbians, though they were undoubtedly intimate. Certainly a good number of fictional texts from the fin de siècle articulated a level of same-sex desire, which goes well beyond the spiritual, but lesbian love in the field of discourse did not exist.

19th century medicine distinguished between "'normal' women's reproductive instincts and 'abnormal' (women's) sexual activities, which were to be treated by surgeons (see above). Medical thinking defined women's sexuality exclusively in relation to heterosexuality."[34] Discourses on lesbianism began to develop in Britain from the 1890s on. Men in the late 19th century felt that love between women became a threat to the social structure. 'Harmless' romantic friendships were discursively transformed into 'unnatural' lesbian relationships.

"Female same-sex desire was linked with anatomical deformity"[35] which fostered the belief in society, that active homosexual behavior could not be carried out by 'normal' and respectable women. In anti-feminist literature, women who 'acted like men', who worked and dressed like men, were labeled the 'intermediate' sex or 'butch' and cast as masculine types who entered in sexual contest with men for feminine women. These women were defined by sexologists of the time as women "who assumes all the negative characteristics of which she accuses the other sex[36]" and "cast as male impostor(s) and sexually voracious predator(s)."[37] 'Feminine' lesbians on the other hand were called 'femmes' and labeled "pseudohomosexual"[38] by sexologists.

The famous British doctor, sexual psychologist and social reformer Havelock Ellis rooted social gender in biological sexuality. His book *Sexual Inversion* (1897) was one of the first works on homosexuality. His theory was that lesbians could be divided into two categories; they were either 'inverts' or 'perverts'. Inverts were in his opinion powerless to change their deviant sexuality because their anomaly was genetic and therefore inborn. Perverts on the other hand had a degree of choice as far as homosexuality was concerned. They possessed a genetic predisposition because of which they could be tempted to enter a lesbian relationship if they were to find themselves in an unwholesome environment, like a women's boarding school or college, a settlement house, a women' club, or a political organization. If such a

---

[33] Heilmann, Ann. *New woman fiction*: women writing first-wave feminism, S. 90
[34] Heilmann, Ann. *New woman fiction*: women writing first-wave feminism, S.129
[35] Heilmann, Ann. *New woman fiction*: women writing first-wave feminism, S128
[36] Heilmann, Ann. *New woman fiction*: women writing first-wave feminism, S.100
[37] Heilmann, Ann. *New woman fiction*: women writing first-wave feminism, S.100
[38]Heilmann, Ann. *New woman fiction*: women writing first-wave feminism, S.99

woman was to be brought up safely in a heterosexual world, she would be able to overcome her lesbian predisposition and grow up to be a "normal", i.e. heterosexual, woman. The connection of advanced education for women and middle-class female homosexuality were certainly counterproductive to the New Women's cause. Nevertheless the simple statement that homosexuality indeed existed (and had a name) opened up a discursive space for lesbian sexuality. The topic now could be talked about and discussed in public in hitherto unknown ways.

Anti-feminist writers often showed their antipathy of feminism through anti-lesbianism topics. To contradict them, feminist writers stressed that their heroines' decision to leave their husbands for a community of women had nothing to do with their sexual preference. They radically destabilized the concept of heterosexuality by making their lesbians into convinced heterosexual women who turn to other women because of the behavior of their husbands.[39] Feminist tried to avoid that their fight for social and economic independence would submerge into a debate about supposed female 'perversion'.

Lesbianism was rarely a subject of lesbian writers themselves but more of anti-feminist writers and scientific studies. The woman-centeredness of much of the literature of the fin de siècle can be read in radical lesbian terms: "as long as patriarchy socializes women into heterosexuality, encouraging them to regard each other as rivals and discouraging female bonding, women's friendship constitutes a form of lesbian (woman-centred) interaction, irrespective of whether this includes actual sexual contact."[40] "The lesbian theme was fraught with difficulties for feminist writers, partly because even those who developed it against the background of anti-feminist and anti-lesbian fiction and sexology, remained ultimately caught between the utopian idea of egalitarian sisterhood and the power-dynamics of woman-to-woman relationships which all too often replicated patriarchal hegemonies."[41]

Homosexuality had seldom been a theme for the feminist movement and New Women in general preferred to focus on civic and constitutional issues rather than on debates surrounding gender and sexuality. Therefore many feminists must have been startled and bewildered to discover that by the turn of the century their campaigns for civic and constitutional rights were being associated with lesbian sexuality.

---

[39] see: Heilmann, Ann. *New woman fiction*: women writing first-wave feminism
[40] Heilmann, Ann. *New woman fiction*: women writing first-wave feminism, S.104
[41] Heilmann, Ann. *New woman fiction*: women writing first-wave feminism, S.108

8. Conclusion

The phenomenon of women who came out of their subordinate, restrictive, and silent corners in order to speak out about problems, support themselves, develop occupational options, and enter the artistic canon, is rightly titled "New Woman movement". The participating women were audacious in their behaviour and demands; women of the 'old stock' were decisively against any changes of traditional roles or conventions. Conservative reactions were often harshly criticising these women who talked about sexual matters and diseases, and claimed citizen as well as distinctively female rights. The literary canon was full of texts by male writers, had male heroes, was written from a male perspective and for a male audience. With the increasing interest of women in literacy and consequently also in literature, new spaces were being opened up. Female writers overthrew literary traditions in order to talk about urgently felt matters from a different and, for the reason of canonical exclusion that hitherto subjected women writers to conformity or silence, also an entirely new point of view. The (re-)claiming of rights for women that covered the whole range from life-changing matters such as marriage and divorce laws to past-time favorites that signified a greater amount of freedom, e.g. bicycle-riding or smoking, was never before acted out by so many different women. Progressive organisations for and by women helped to bring about cultural and judicial adjustments that enabled women to at least get a taste of the new century's liberty.

Sources

Boris, Eileen. *Complicating categories : gender, class, race and ethnicity.* Cambridge:
  Cambridge University Press, 1999
Bourke, Joanna. *Working-class cultures in Britain 1890-1960 : gender, class, and ethnicity.*
  London: Routledge, 1994
Dahlerup, Drude (ed.). *The new women's movement : feminism and political. power in Europe
  and the USA.* London: Sage, 1986
Daly, Nicholas. *Modernism, romance and the Fin de siècle: popular fiction and British
  culture, 1880- 1914.* Cambridge: Cambridge University Press, 1999
Gagen, Jean Elisabeth. *The New Woman - Her emergence in English drama, 1600-1730.* New
  York: Twayne, 1954
Gardner, Viv (ed.). *The new woman and her sisters: feminism and theatre 1850 – 1914.*New
  York: Harvester Wheatsheaf, 1992
Heilmann, Ann. *New woman fiction: women writing first-wave feminism.* Basingstoke:
  Macmillan, 2000
Hoffmann, Gerhard. *Postmodernism and the Fin de Siècle.* Heidelberg: Winter, 2002
Ledger, Sally. *The New Woman: Fiction and Feminism at the Fin de Siècle.* Manchester:
  Manchester University Press, 1997
Ledger, Sally. *The fin de siècle : a reader in cultural history, c. 1880-1900.* Oxford: Oxford
  University Press, 2000
Marks, Patricia. *Bicycles, bangs, and bloomers : the new woman in the popular press.*
  Lexington: University Press of Kentucky, 1990
Nelson, Carolyn (ed.). *A New Woman Reader: Fiction, Articles, Drama of the 1890s.*
  Christensen: Broadview Press, 2000
Richardson, Angelique (ed.). *The New Woman in Fiction and in Fact: Fin-de-Siècle
  Feminisms.* Basingstoke [u.a.]: Palgrave [u.a.], 2001.
Showalter, Elaine. *Sexual anarchy : gender and culture at the Fin de Siècle.* London: Virago,
  1996

http://www.litencyc.com/php/stopics.php?rec=true&UID=3
http://www.wwnorton.com/nael/victorian/topic_2/new.htm
http://www.nwe.ufl.edu/~jdouglas/litprop.pdf
http://www.broadviewpress.com/bvbooks.asp?BookID=670
http://hwj.oxfordjournals.org/cgi/content/abstract/56/1/33
http://www.fathom.com/course/10701039/session4.html
http://www.tudorlinks.com/treasury/articles/view1890.html
http://www.historylearningsite.co.uk/suffragettes.htm   all August, 2005